CO-AMY-765

A detail from a painting by a Sister
of the Community of St. Mary
Used with the kind permission of
the Reverend Mother Superior

A detail from a painting by a Sister
of the Community of St. Mary.
Used with the kind permission of
the Reverend Mother Superior.

THE INFANT KING

THE MYSTERIES OF CHRISTMAS
IN MEDITATION

BY

Shirley C. Hughson, O. H. C.

GEN. THEO. SEMINARY LIBRARY

HOLY CROSS PRESS
WEST PARK, N. Y.
1920

Lit

76539   *4644.04*

CONTENTS

THE INFANT KING

CHRISTMAS EVE

"While all things were in quiet silence, and night was in the midst of her swift course, Thine Almighty Word leaped down from Heaven out of Thy royal throne."—Wisdom 18:14, 15.

I. "STAND YE STILL AND SEE THE SALVATION OF THE LORD." (Exod. 14:13).

1. Take note of those to whom the revelation of the coming Lord was given. It was to those who waited for redemption in Jerusalem. God's Church had become corrupt, but the Church was greater than the hierarchy that for the time controlled its outward activities. There were those who knew the promises of God, and their faith staggered not, though the time was long and weary.

2. Picture those who knew of the approaching day. First, the Holy Mother, rapt through these long nine months in a wondering awe, as she felt

1

within her womb the precious burden of her God and her Son. With what thrill of expectancy did she greet the day of days! St. Joseph, whose confidence had been reassured by the Angel, how he longed and waited as the months passed, to see the salvation of Israel. St. Elisabeth, with the infant Baptist at her aged breast, how she waited, as the time drew near, to hear news of that Blessed Mother. In our time the Church is hard-pressed. We have the same precious promises. Does our faith fail not?

II. THE MESSAGE OF REDEMPTION CAN ONLY COME TO THOSE WHOSE HEARTS ARE ATTUNED TO HEAR.

1. Consider the shepherds on the hills, and the multitude of the heavenly host praising God. How loud their anthem sounded across the world, but men did not hear. Only the humble shepherds caught the vision and heard the angel-song.

2. It requires a trained ear to catch the more delicate tones of an orchestra. There are notes in nature the vibrations of which are so rapid that only a few have a sense of hearing keen enough to perceive them. So with the voices with which God speaks to us. We must train our ears to hearken, or the highest messages from God will be lost. Am I hearkening what the Lord God will say?

III. Sorrow on Earth; Joy in Heaven.

1. Consider the silence of the night covering the sorrows of the world; God's people under a foreign yoke; the Shekinah departed from the temple; the holy people scattered abroad; and they loved to have it so. A few faithful souls, whose tears ran down day and night for Israel; a crying from a few hearts for light and redemption. Hold fast, brave hearts,— "to-morrow ye shall have help, saith the Lord of Hosts."

2. Consider the sorrow at Bethlehem.

The blustering winter evening drawing in; the darkness coming on; the weary travellers pleading for shelter from house to house; door after door closed against them. "He came unto His own, and His own received Him not." "He had not where to lay His Head." Then the stable, the manger, the Virgin Mother, the troubled old man, the lantern dimly burning, an infant shivering with the cold, an infant crying in the night. And that Infant is God. But be of good courage,—"To-day ye shall know that the Lord will come, and in the morning ye shall see His glory."

3. God's redemption draweth nigh. A vision of Angels; a message to breathless, awe-struck shepherds;—"unto you is born this day in the city of David a Saviour which is Christ the Lord;" a mighty strain of celestial harmony: "Glory to God in the highest, on earth peace to men of good will." The Joy of God has come down to earth. To

them that fear His Name hath the Sun of Righteousness arisen, with healing in His wings. "To-morrow ye shall have help, to-morrow the iniquity of the earth shall be done away."

CHRISTMAS DAY

Read St. Luke 2:1-20.

I. THE HOLY BIRTH.

1. "No room for them in the inn." Room for everything else but the Saviour of the world. Time and place for business, for pleasure, family reunions as the people came up from all parts of the country; but no room for Jesus. More serious souls talked, doubtless, of the hope of Israel, but when He knocked at the door there was no room. Consider the inn as the picture of my heart. Shall I make room for Jesus there?

2. Pass from the light and warmth of the inn to the cold and desolation of the stable. No good cheer there, no laughter, no glad greetings of love; only the darkness of the night, the winter wind, the rough manger, the silent cattle,

the cold stars shining in the midnight sky. But there was a joy deeper, tenser, than ever human heart had felt before, for Jesus our God was here. For the first time since the catastrophe of Eden the eyes of man looked upon God. The happy Virgin Mother, the joy of aged Joseph, the Holy Child at the Mother's breast,—here was God and the Blessed Saints, here was heaven. Kneel in this place, adoring your Saviour and your God.

II. THE ANGEL VISITANTS.

1. No room in the inn, no room in the hearts of men, but messengers of God heralded the divine birth. The faithful shepherds on the hills—the sudden blaze of angelic glory—the glorious message: "Unto you is born this day a Saviour;"— the midnight sky all full of shining forms.

2. But alas for the sin of man! Even the most faithful, the holy chosen ones are made afraid of God through sin.

The blameless Zacharias at the temple altar, the holy Virgin at Nazareth, the shepherds of Bethlehem,—they were sore afraid. No room in the hearts of sinners, and fear in the hearts of the holy ones. This is what the God of love finds when He would come to save His people. When again He comes, will my heart shrink back in fear? When again He comes, will my heart leap up in love?

3. "Glory to God in the highest." God finding glory in His own humiliation, in His own destitution. Manger and straw, Angels and stars, wind and cold, light and darkness,—all work together to minister to the divine honour; and the Holy Mother summons all creation to sing with her its *Benedicite* in praise of her God and her Son. Hear the Virgin softly singing as she rocks her Baby on her breast: "O ye Angels of the Lord, bless ye the Lord; O ye stars of heaven, bless ye the Lord; O ye winds of

God, bless ye the Lord; O ye frost and cold, bless ye the Lord; O ye light and darkness, bless ye the Lord; praise Him and magnify Him forever."

III. THE SHEPHERDS.

1. Fainter grows the angel-song; the last shining form sinks out of sight behind the stars; again the silent night. The shepherds look one upon another. Fear yields to a longing to look upon the Blessed One Who has come to redeem and save. The energy of love conquers fear. "Let us now go even unto Bethlehem and see this thing which is come to pass."

2. The spirit of the coming Kingdom had entered into their hearts. Consider how it is illustrated in their words: "*Let us*,"—the unity of action based on love; no rivalry for the honour of greeting the Saviour. "*Now*,"—no delay; "Now is the accepted time, now is the day of Salvation." "*Go*,"—love inciting to action;

doing something for God. *"Even unto Bethlehem,"*—even the little obscure city, to seek for a King, not in a royal palace, but in a manger; to find God in the humble things of life.

3. "And they came with haste, and found Mary, and Joseph, and the babe lying in a manger." In the lowly place, which they sought in obedience to the heavenly vision, they found God and the blessed Saints. Let us kneel to-day before the crib; here shall we find the type of the highest glory and happiness the Kingdom can offer us, a foretaste of Heaven,—participation in the worship of Incarnate God in the Communion of Saints.

THE INFANT KING

DECEMBER 26.

ST. STEPHEN'S DAY

I. CONSIDER INCARNATE GOD AS A LIT-
TLE BABY IN THE MANGER; AND INCAR-
NATE GOD ENTHRONED IN HIGHEST
HEAVEN STANDING TO SUCCOUR THOSE
WHO CALL ON HIM.

1. See St. Stephen, powerless before
the council. They are able to wreak
their wicked will on him. God was within him, and yet God permitted his enemies to have their way. He led him
through the experience of weakness, of
helplessness, in order that he might
share His glory, His power, His throne.

2. Consider St. Stephen as like to our
Lord in His Nativity and in His Passion.
Angels behold the wondrous Birth, and
yet the Infant God flees for His life.
Twelve legions of angels would have saved
Him from the soldiers in the Garden, but

11

He puts aside all help and goes forth to die. "Suffer it to be so now."

3. Consider St. Stephen as like our Lord in glory. Glory out of humiliation; strength out of weakness. His following Christ in the path of humiliation and death led to his exaltation with Him. But it was not the mere actual persecution that gave him his crown. It was his glad willingness to follow wherever Jesus might lead. "I will get me to the mountain of myrrh," cried the Wise Man of old; but he knew that the way of patient suffering led to the Delectable Mountains, where crowns, and the joy of heavenly worship were waiting; and so he added like a triumph cry:—"and to the hill of frankincense."

II. THE MARTYRS OF GOD.

1. In one sense, we are all called to be martyrs. The daily trial is that under which we are to humble ourselves that we might be exalted. The trial will come

in any case. It comes to all, good and bad alike. Do I receive it willingly, recognizing it as a portion of the True Cross laid on my heart?

2. How often the joyful side of religion attracts, while the suffering repels. I run to sing with the Angels under the glowing midnight stars; I draw back from the darkness and cold of the stable. St. Stephen cried aloud for joy at the vision of his Lord, but he also rejoiced in dying for the same Lord. "The stones of the torrent were sweet to him."

III. THE GLORY THAT IS TO COME.

1. "Wherefore God hath highly exalted him and given him a name." These words, spoken first of Christ, apply equally to every humble martyr of Christ. *Wherefore*, i. e., because we have suffered with Him we shall reign, and He will give us a new name in His Kingdom.

2. Consider the name Stephen. The word means *a crown*. The Scripture tells

us the faithful are as the jewels of God,
to be gathered up at the end of the world.
St. Paul calls his beloved Philippians
his "Joy and crown." So the faithful
souls will be our Lord's crown of rejoicing. They will beautify and adorn the
Kingdom. The Prophet declares: "Thou
shalt also be a crown of glory in the Hand
of the Lord, and a royal diadem in the
Hand of thy God." (Isa. 62:3).

3. Consider how St. Stephen became
a crown in the hand of the Lord. (*a*) He
was "Full of Faith and of the Holy
Ghost;" by earnest labour he strength-
ened himself in faith and the gifts of the
Spirit. (*b*) He had been studious to
know the truth of God, as he showed in
his defense. (*c*) By courage in time of
adversity, (*d*) by patience under persecution, (*e*) by a perfect trust in God,
(*f*) by forgiving his enemies, (*g*) by
praying for them after the manner of his
Lord. Let me examine myself by these

and other like considerations drawn from
the history of the martyr to see if I am
seeking to become my Lord's crown of
rejoicing.

ST. JOHN'S DAY

I. OUR LORD'S TRAINING OF THE BE-
LOVED DISCIPLE.

1. The call: "Not yours but you"
(II Cor. 12:14). They "left the ship and
their father and followed Him" (St.
Matt. 4:22). "He that loveth father or
mother more than Me is not worthy of
Me" (St. Matt. 10:37). Our Lord
stripped him in the beginning. No
gradual loosening of the ties of affection.
"Get thee out of thy country and from
thy kindred and from thy father's house"
(Gen. 12:1). "Forget also thine own
people" (Ps. 45:10). Is this the literal
quality of my response? If not, do I
expect God to receive me?

2. "As many as I love, I rebuke and
chasten" (Rev. 3:19). How often our
Lord rebuked the Beloved Disciple. "Ye

know not what ye ask,"—when he sought to be closest to Him in His kingdom. He rebuked them and said, "Ye know not what manner of spirit ye are of" (St. Luke 9:55). Thus was His special love to him manifested. Thus did He train him to be worthy of the highest vision. His love could not bear to see the imperfections in His beloved. Consider the rebukes I suffer. What lies behind them? For what is my Lord preparing me? Do I resent His loving training and refuse to be led along the way of discipline?

II. St. John the Type of the Perfect Christian.

1. His Obedience (the all-comprehending virtue), even to the limiting of the exercise of his apostolic ministry. All the other Apostles imperilled their lives daily in savage lands for the Gospel's sake. St. John remained, in obedience to God's will, in security at Jerusalem or Ephesus. Year by year came the

news of glorious martyrdoms. How small in comparison seemed his sufferings for Christ!

2. Picture the scene at the Latin Gate. The day, it seemed, had come when the privilege of martyrdom was to be his. History tells us how the Apostle was cast into the boiling caldron by the heathen persecutor, but the power of God brought him forth unhurt, the crown held within reach was snatched away. This honour was not to be his, though he had lain on the Lord's breast at Supper. He had once asked to be given a lofty place in the completed Kingdom, but the lesson that he learned as he lay so near the Sacred Heart was, not to long for crowns of glory, or place of honour, but only for the will of God wherein was his peace.

III. The School of Submission to God's Will.

1. St. John learned what we must learn, that a busy, fruitful ministry is not

the highest offering to God; nor yet perils by land or sea, or even life yielded up in martyrdom. His was the highest call and privilege,—to offer his will, to do the humble work, even to be forgotten of men for Christ's sake. After Pentecost he is mentioned only twice in the Acts, and then only as St. Peter's companion. St. Paul in his fourteen epistles mentions him but once.

2. Because with a strong will he had mastered his lesson, to him was given the vision of the Lord in glory. But the vision vouchsafed to the Beloved Disciple on Patmos is in no wise more glorious than that which the future holds for each of us, provided we, too, learn our lessons of Christ. Watch for the lesson of to-day. Submit to be taught of God; and mark it as a pledge of the vision that will some day be yours.

THE HOLY INNOCENTS' DAY

I. THE SORROWS OF THE INCARNATION.

1. Consider the grief of the Heart of Incarnate God that His coming should have brought grief to so many souls. In the Annunciation, the Holy Virgin is troubled at the Angel's saying. The Incarnation brings only a terrible suspicion to the mind of the holy Joseph. The Shepherds are sore afraid; and now His birth in the city of His Fathers brings the murder of helpless infants, broken hearts to many mothers, terror and desolation to the whole city.

2. It is not so hard to suffer for those we love. But how great a grief when we cause suffering to them. Think of the sudden midnight flight; of the Infant Christ clinging to His Mother's breast;

and in His ears the cries of little children
slain by a cruel tyrant.

3. He came to save and deliver. His
coming brought death and heart-desola-
tion. The Cross was planted firmly in
His path at the outset of His life, the
hardest cross of all to bear, that others
should die for Him Who came to die for
them.

II. THE OVERRULING LOVE OF GOD.

1. The love of God out of grief and
terror brought glory and joy. Consider
Holman Hunt's picture of the Flight into
Egypt, the Infant Christ accompanied
to the land of exile by the souls of the
Innocents, radiant with everlasting joy,
sweeping on in triumphal procession with
celestial songs, a guard of honour to their
Infant King.

2. Let us hear the voice of the Beloved: "They shall obtain joy and gladness, and sorrow and sighing shall flee
away" (Isa. 35:10). Let us see in every

disappointment, every grief or annoyance, the raw material of our eternal rejoicing, if we offer them to Him in patience and love.

III. THE DIVINE PERMISSION OF EVIL.

1. For the sanctifying of the Saints God permits evil and sin in the world. Evil angels, evil men, all are forced, in spite of their own intentions, to contribute to the divine glory. Consider Satan in impotent rage as he sees the efforts of his infernal emissaries resulting only in the building up of the walls of the eternal Kingdom.

2. Select for consideration some of the things that hurt and worry you. See in them "the blow and biting sculpture" by which you are being fashioned as an elect stone for the upbuilding of the celestial Kingdom. Are you willing to endure it all for God's honour in the perfecting of your soul?

3. These considerations must rejoice us and fill us with great gratitude. Make a definite act of thanksgiving for some of the things that annoy you to-day. Contrast the Innocents of Bethlehem growing up amid the sin and sorrow of the world, with their souls now going in triumph as the royal body-guard of the King of Kings. Which condition is to be desired? Apply the answer to your own life, to your own burdens and trials.

THE WORSHIPPERS AT THE CRIB

I. THE HOLY MOTHER.

1. Consider Mary looking for the first time upon the Face of her divine Son, and bowing down in humble adoration. She had for nine months borne Him in her womb, her heart in adoration of Him day and night. Now she sees Him face to face.

2. Her worship of her unborn Son was the type of my worship in this life when God is hidden from my eyes. When I see Him face to face I shall join in the heavenly worship with our Holy Mother. Faithfulness here will bring me this reward in the glory of the Beatific Vision.

3. He regarded the lowliness of His handmaiden. A realization of the Pres-

ence of God brings humility. Pride, the root of all sin, cannot lift up its horrid head if I realize God is with me. The holy, humble Mother of God, realizing her Lord, her God and her Son, is the type of humility to which I must try to conform. If hour by hour I realize His presence, I will by His Presence be able to slay the proud spirit within me.

II. St. Joseph.

1. Consider what must have been the holiness of him whom God chose to be the witness of this mystery, making him the foster-father of the Incarnate Son. Meditate on the holiness of him whom God condescended to reassure in his hour of awful doubt by the message of an angel, and who, next to the Mother of God, was held worthy to look on the Face of God, and bow down and worship Him in the Flesh.

2. Consider St. Joseph's response to grace. All his long life yielding to the constant and progressive calling of the

Spirit, with every avenue between his heart and God wide open, unobstructed by any wilful sin. Meditate on the floods of grace he received during these nine mysterious months. Consider the influence of the company of Mary, the atmosphere of the continual presence of Incarnate God, his silent communion with the angels who guarded that Holy Thing and His Blessed Mother. This holy companionship is mine in the Communion of Saints if I too keep the avenues of my heart open to God.

III. THE HOLY SHEPHERDS.

1. Their hiddenness. Like St. Joseph, their previous history is unknown. No hint of name or family or tribe. Only one thing is known of them before the angelic vision: viz. they were keeping their flocks, doing their duty in that state of life to which it had pleased God to call them.

2. Without further introduction we are told that these obscure men have a

vision of angels; heavenly visitants converse with them; they are given to hear heavenly anthems, to see the Christmas skies full of the shining messengers of God. They receive the first announcement of the glorious news; they are sent to find Him; to them is accorded the honour of being the first preachers of Christ, filling with wondering awe the hearts of those to whom they told these glorious and heavenly things.

3. Their earthly history is a blank. This one incident, and the obscurity closes about them again. But their spiritual history we know. We can reconstruct it point by point: their humility, faithfulness to duty, ever deepening love of God and man, their life of prayer and communion, patiently waiting on Him,—the light of that one Night reveals these and a hundred other things belonging to their spiritual history. What will the light of the Second Coming reveal in me?

THE PONDERING OF MARY

"But Mary kept all these things, and pondered them in her heart."—St. Luke 2:19.

I. THE BLESSED MOTHER IN MEDITATION.

1. Picture her meditation at Nazareth on the night of the Incarnation. Tradition tells us that she was meditating on the words of the Prophet, "A virgin shall conceive and bear a son" (Isa. 7:14). In her humility she did not connect the mysterious words with herself. But all heaven stood on tiptoe in breathless waiting for this supreme moment, when her response, "Be it unto me according to thy word," was to speak the greatest of mysteries into existence.

2. By her simple word of submission she was to institute, as it were, the new worship for the angelic hosts which had

been promised them of old,—the worship of God made man: "When He bringeth in the first-begotten into the world, He saith, And let all the Angels of God worship Him" (Heb. 1:6). And yet all unconscious was she of the mighty honour that God had in store for her, such was the humility of her simple heart.

3. But the knowledge of the Incarnation has given us a higher and more glorious truth than could have then been known, even by the holy Virgin Mother. So let me not meditate on the truths and mysteries of God as something apart from myself. If I am knit up into Christ I am caught up into the operation of every truth, every mystery. No thought or action of the Divine Head but affects essentially every member of the Body. The Head shares all things with the Body. This day He is preparing some miracle of grace to which I am to give force and efficacy by correspondence with His call, even perhaps in this meditation.

II. The Faith of Mary in Medita-
TION.

1. She could not yet understand the
mystery of this wondrous birth, of the
strange certainty within her that her
little Child was God the Redeemer, of the
Shepherd's adoration, and the song of the
Angels which she had heard far above the
hills. But she did not ask to be en-
lightened save by an increase of faith.
She took these strange mysteries into
her heart and pondered them there, learn-
ing more and more of the truth as she
worshipped.

2. Faith brought knowledge; humble
worship made clear the vision. If I
accepted all that God sent me, with some-
what of her faith, the perplexities of life
would pass away. Not that my limited
little mind could compass the mysteries
of God or even those of my own life, but
I would know how not to worry. Perplexity would vanish. I would become
as the happy-hearted little child to whom

it does not occur to ask the reason why, but goes forward with eagerness and gladness to do the will of a father she loves and trusts, thinking only of the faithful doing, not of the results.

III. MARY GUARDING HER HEART.

1. She *kept* all these things in her heart, we are told. She guarded them well as precious gifts from God. She allowed no other interests to enter in and thrust them out. No subtle suggestion from the tempter could make her for a moment forget the precious truth that had been confided to her.

2. Consider her as the second Eve tempted by the serpent. See her spurn his suggestions from her mind. She stops not to consider for a moment what he says. No question arises in her thoughts. Her eyes have seen, her hands have handled, and no vision of the tempter can draw her from the contemplation of this perfect Vision that is hers.

3. Consider the wonderful things God has said to me, the glorious revelation that has been given to my heart. And yet, how easily it becomes obscured. How quickly am I distracted from the heavenly things that have been committed to my trust. I forget them in the midst of my meditations, my Communion, my prayers. Every passing thing clouds my thought and obscures the vision of Jesus.

THE END OF THE YEAR

I. THE BURDEN OF THE PAST.

1. How heavy it lies upon our hearts. So much to regret, so much lost that will never come again. Other opportunities, other graces, but these nevermore. Recount some of the greatest of these opportunities and reflect how little we have made of them. Cry, *Mea culpa, mea maxima culpa.*

2. Consider (*a*) what has been lost to self, and (*b*) what has been lost to the honour of God. We had our own salvation to work out with fear and trembling. We had His Holy Name to glorify. Is our salvation nearer? Have we made His Name one of praise as we walked among men? We can only cry, *Peccavi.*

3. But the cry *Peccavi*, the cry *Mea culpa*, arouses the blessed God to action.

Who is this calling to Him out of a broken and contrite heart, the heart that He has declared He will not despise? To the cry of penitence, to the desire to make reparation, He answers on the swift feet of love. The heart that is bowed down in penitence He will cleanse and renew; the heart that cries to Him in sorrow for sin is the heart He will equip anew and send forth to repair the breaches its own failings have made. With a great forgiving love He trusts it again to retrieve its own losses, and to build again the places of His honour that have been broken down. Let us leave the old year with a great act of penitence, and turn to the new year with hearts renewed in grace and power and joy.

II. "BEHOLD I MAKE ALL THINGS NEW."

1. Every old year dies amidst the glory of the light of the Incarnation. The end of a year is a solemn, but not a sorrowful occasion. Old things are done away, but God gives us the pledge of new

opportunities which we shall be able to improve if we trust in the power of the Incarnate Life that dwells in our hearts.

2. So with every new year comes renewed opportunity, and this means increased responsibility, and increased accountability. We shrink from the stern account that has to be rendered. Is it because we are too unwilling or too slothful to lay hold of, and like the Blessed Mother, guard and conserve, the precious gifts of His own power which the Christ Child has committed to us?

3. The failures of the past year depress us. We ask our hearts if we can do any better in the coming months. If we depend on self, No. But can we now depend on self? We have been to Bethlehem, we have heard the angel-song, and the message glorious; we have hastened with the shepherds to the manger-throne, we have seen the Virgin Mother, the new-born Child, and have worshipped Him

as He lay upon that Mother's breast. With these things so lately come to us we have no fear for the coming months. He will go with us in joy or sorrow, in trial or victory. The prayers of the Blessed Mother, and of the Blessed Angels, will be offered on our behalf. We face the future with gladness and strength because we have knelt with the holy ones at Bethlehem.

JANUARY 1.

THE HOLY NAME

"Thou shalt call His Name Jesus, for He shall save His people from their sins."—St. Matthew 1:21.

I. THE SIGNIFICANCE OF THE HOLY NAME.

1. The word *Jesus* means *Saviour*. The Name which was given Him by the Angel "before He was conceived in the womb," testified of the great redeeming work He was come to do. Twice did the Angel foretell His Name: once to the Blessed Mother, once to St. Joseph. Thus twice was the heavenly pledge given that the redemption of Israel was at hand. Consider the divine goodness that thus rejoiced to give this blessed assurance to the longing hearts of His holy ones.

2. He was to save His people from what? From sin. Nothing is said of a

saving from condemnation and from hell.
These were, in a sense, secondary objects
of His coming. His mission was pri-
marily to save them from sin *now*; not
at some future time from judgment and
hell, which are the fruits of sin. Am I
permitting Him to save me *now*? To
save me from the power of the evil that
is to-day in my life; or that to-day is seeking to ensnare me?

3. If I am yielding myself now to His
saving power I need have no fear of judgment and hell. If I give myself to His
daily progressive work of saving me from
my sins, there will be nothing in me that
will be subject to condemnation, nothing
in me that will offer fuel for the fires of
hell. "O Jesus, be Thou my Jesus."

II. THE OPERATION OF HIS SAVING
POWER.

1. Not only does He save from the
snare and stain of actual sin, but from
the effects of forgiven sin as they remain

in the soul. He is content with no soul being barely saved. He longs to lead us on to ever higher things, to ever nobler achievement, to ever subtler and more precious graces in His Kingdom. Such is the predestination He has prepared for me from eternity.

2. Let us in sorrow and shame compare our spiritual ambitions for ourselves with His ambition for us. We are content to keep out of mortal sin, admitting venial sins even habitually; indulging numberless imperfections with no serious effort even to realize what they are,—wounding, dishonouring, grieving Him daily, and content to have it so, if only we escape hell at the last. He, on the other hand, is never content, either in this life or in purgatory, so long as the smallest stain remains; tireless in every possible exercise of Omnipotence to establish, strengthen, settle us; to sanctify and perfect us, to make us meet for the highest place in His Kingdom.

3. Do I permit the power of His saving Name of Jesus to work thus in my life; not content with being cleansed from sin, but with passionate longing seeking to share His own sanctity and perfection? The original purpose of God was not merely to rescue man from sin and evil, for these had no place at all in that original plan. His purpose was to unite man to Himself, to lift him up to the throne of His own glory. This purpose has never wavered. Am I allowing Him thus to be my Saviour, my Jesus? Alas that He should be called Jesus, but be no Jesus of mine!

REJECTED OF MEN

" He came unto His own, and His own received Him not.   But as many as received Him, to them gave He power to become the sons of God."—St. John 1:11, 12.

I. The Lord's Rejection by His Own.

1. Consider His rejection by His own people in His own home.   Think of all that He had done for them; He led them about, He instructed them, He kept them as the apple of His eye (Deut. 32:10). Then as the crowning blessing He came to them in their own flesh, and the doors of Bethlehem closed against Him were the type of the hearts of His people.

2. Is my heart as their hearts? He came to me in mighty love when I was a little child. He led me about, He instructed me; more precious was my soul to Him than the apple of His eye,—yea, than His own soul, for He gave that up in

death for me. Does He now come to me and I receive Him not? Let my life pass in review before me; let me see the goodness and mercy that have followed me all my days; let me ask my soul, What reward dost thou give to the Lord for all the benefits He hath done unto thee?

II. To them gave He Power.

1. It was a free gift, a gift of His love. Man had done nothing to merit it. Indeed in His fallen state, he could do nothing to merit even the smallest gift from God. But the goodness of God does not wait until we deserve it. He only asks us to receive Him, and He will "with Him also freely give us all things" (Rom. 8:32). His Heart sends forth to me this power because He loves me. Repeat over and over again, as you contemplate the Holy Christ in the manger, the words, "Every good gift and every perfect gift is from above, and cometh down from the Father of lights" (St. James 1:17).

Kneel at the manger, and say to the little Child of Bethlehem, "Come to my heart, Lord Jesus; there is room in my heart for Thee."

2. This precious gift of power to become the son of God is not given as though it were some mere spiritual adornment. It is given to be used. "I put thee in remembrance that thou stir up the gift of God which is in thee" (II Tim. 1:6).

III. POWER TO BECOME SONS.

1. He does not make us to be the sons of God apart from our own efforts. If we receive Him He gives us power, i. e., the right, to become the sons of God, but rights fail if they be not exercised.

2. I became a son of God in Baptism; Holy Communion enables me to continue the life of sonship; every Sacrament, every prayer, deepens my relation of sonship to my Father.

3. Rights bring duties. Privileges of sonship involve responsibilities. The good son must be *loyal*; he must be *obedient*; he must be *loving*. When he fails he must be *humble* and *penitent*, and he must seek to repair the Father's honour by *a still more zealous service*. Let me consider what each of these means, and let me examine myself by these tests.

THE SON OF A KING

"Which were born, not of blood, nor of the will of the flesh, nor of the will of man, but of God."—St. John 1:13.

I. "BORN, NOT OF BLOOD."

1. Such is the description of those who receive Him, and to whom, believing on His Name, He gives power to become the sons of God. No mere human descent from a chosen people. True children of Abraham only when true children of God. No pride of birth, or of worldly station. No natural talents or ability derived or fostered by heredity or environment. The true aristocracy of the Kingdom of heaven are born of God one by one, even as the angels were created one by one. My soul will have its place in the kingdom only if I personally use the power that He bestows upon me to become a son of God. And I can maintain this place

only by faithful use of the ordained means of grace.

2. "Nor of the will of the flesh," for "of His own will begat He us with the word of truth" (St. James 1:18). "He is our Father and Mother in One." His will cooperating with the revealed truth, as a father cooperating with a mother, brought us forth as children of the Kingdom. Our wills, indeed, had to cooperate with His, but our wills were powerless without Him. Of ourselves, we could neither claim nor merit the new birth.

3. "Nor of the will of man." He gave to men power indeed to become the sons of God, but this power was received from Him as a free gift. No matter what my strength of purpose, or constancy of will, I have no power to be born into the Kingdom, any more than the nameless germ of life has power to will itself to be born into the world as a man-child.

II. "But of God."

1. We are all "of the Father's love begotten." Meditate upon God's foreknowledge of how I would fail to respond to His love. He knew I would rebel and dishonour Him among men.

2. Why, then, did He not leave me in heathen darkness, and call through this divine birth some worthier soul to be of His children? I know not, save that He loved me and was glad to suffer all dishonour at my hands, if only at the last He could claim me for His own.

3. Consider the mighty stimulus of the recollection that I am born of God. I am His child, the child of a King. I am one of the Princes of the blood royal of the everlasting Kingdom. I must live according to the dignity of a Prince. I can do nothing that would dishonour my royal name and heritage. I must be true to my kingly Father; I must live so as to bring no shame upon my brethren and

kinsfolk in the divine family, even the
Angels and the Saints of God.

4.   Consider the mighty stimulus of
the recollection that I have won the love
of no perishing mortal, but the infinite
love of Him Who is from Everlasting.
He Who had before Him all the best of
all the ages upon which to set His Heart,
chose me.

THE INFANT GOD

"Whom saw ye, shepherds, say, tell us; Who hath appeared in the earth? We saw the new-born Child and the choirs of angels praising the Lord together."—Antiphon for Christmas.

I. "WHOM SAW YE?"

1. He Whom the shepherds saw and worshipped was Very God of Very God, Omnipotent, Omniscient. By Him all things were made. By Him all things are sustained. Perfect God lies in the manger as a little Infant, in humiliation and destitution receiving the homage of His creatures. They who would be exalted with Him must follow Him in His lowliness. "Learn of Me for I am meek and lowly in heart,"—this is the first lesson Incarnate God inculcates in the hearts of His worshippers.

2. He Whom the shepherds saw was "perfect Man of a reasonable soul and

human flesh subsisting." They saw God in humiliation, but they saw man in exaltation—manhood taken up into the Godhead. They saw their own destiny. Those who accept Christ in His humiliation, and being joined to Him in Baptism, members of His Body, have only to maintain, (as He will give them the ability), this oneness. Being united with Him they cannot but follow Him, and so will they enter with Him into His glory.

3. He Whom the shepherds saw was at the same time both God and Man. The Person of God the Eternal Son, maintaining all that was eternally His of the divine Nature and attributes, became Man of the substance of the Virgin Mary, taking all that belonged to complete Manhood, becoming one with us in all things, sin only excepted. With the burden of sin that lay upon us we could not rise up to God; so He came down to us to take our nature to Himself, and to perfect it, and thus to make us who pos-

sess this nature worthy of eternal union with Him.

II. "THE NEW-BORN CHILD AND THE CHOIRS OF ANGELS PRAISING THE LORD TOGETHER."

1. Contemplate the new-born Child leading the choirs of the Angels. Now for the first time since the Fall of Adam does Man give perfect praise to God. Hearken to that mighty Voice sounding aloud amidst the angelic ranks, rallying them to perfect praise: "O ye Angels of the Lord, Bless ye the Lord: O ye Powers of the Lord, Bless ye the Lord, Praise Him and magnify Him forever." Hear the responding anthem of the heavenly host: "Glory to God in the highest, and on earth peace to men of good-will."

2. Not only to the angel choirs does the voice of the God-Man call. To us and to all creation comes the summons: "O all ye works of the Lord, Bless ye the Lord: O ye children of men, Bless ye the

Lord: Praise Him and magnify Him forever."

3. Only by union with Him can I join this choir of perfect praise. Sin makes this union impossible, for "what communion hath light with darkness?" (II Cor. 6:14). The purpose of my creation is that I might take my place in this choir of praise. This purpose is eternally baulked if I flee not from sin. Flee, then, O my soul, from evil, and "follow after righteousness, godliness, faith, love, patience, meekness" (I Tim. 6:11). Then will the eternal union, then will the perfect praise, be thine.

THE PRECIOUS BLOOD

I. "THE CIRCUMCISING OF THE CHILD"
  (St. Luke 2:21).

1. Our Lord's Circumcision presents
the principle that underlay His whole
life. This rite was that which brought
the child into the divine Covenant.
But He, being God, did not need to be
brought into the Covenant. Yet He
submitted to Circumcision. It was not
the mere letter of the law with which He
was complying. It was a submission
to the principle of obedience.

2. His Circumcision was the first
shedding of the Precious Blood. This
was the pledge of the obedience unto
death, even that death of the Cross in
which He poured out the full flood of the
Precious Blood for the life of the world.
He had come to be the Holocaust, to give

Himself to the uttermost, and He would not shrink from the pain of this offering of the few precious drops, even though in strictness He could not be subject to this demand of the law. I offer myself to God a holocaust in obedience. Do I shrink back from some slight subjection of my will because perhaps no formal obedience is laid upon me?

3. "I came not to do mine own will but the will of Him that sent me" (St. John 6:38). Note the sequence of the two parts of this sentence. First, the denying of His own will. Then, His human will being set aside, the doing of the will of God following easily and surely. He, indeed, needed no mortification of His human will, which was of necessity at one with the divine will; yet for our further instruction He sets forth in this sentence the same principle that He had declared in submitting to circumcision.

4. So we mortify our wills not as an end in itself, but that we might do the

divine will. The work is not completed
with self-mortification. This would issue
in pride. Self-mortification only clears
the way, and gets all in readiness for what
He, through the Holy Spirit, would work
within us.

II. "THE BLOOD IS THE LIFE" (Deut.
12:23).

1. For love of me He shed His Precious Blood, thus giving His life for me.
He may not ask me to shed my blood for
Him, but none the less does He demand
love for love and life for life. I lay it
down for Him not in dying but in living;
not in sacrifice once for all, but in the
sacrifice day by day of my will to Him.
This is what my baptismal obligation in-
volves.

2. His sacrifice for me was the fruit
of His love. My sacrifice will be a worthless thing if behind it lies not love. Service for selfish ends, for the saving of my
own soul; service even because, nursed

in the Faith, common sense dictates it as the only reasonable course,—all these He may accept, but not unless the motive of my love is stronger than them all. The First Commandment is: "Thou shalt love the Lord thy God."

3. All this means that He desires the service of sons, not of hirelings or slaves. We cannot buy the privileges and rewards of the Kingdom with our service, nor claim them even as the slaves of duty. They are His free and loving gifts. He who would lay down his life in the truest service thinks not of the gifts but of the Giver. And we love Him, not for reward but for Himself. "We love Him because He first loved us" (I St. John 4:19).

THE EPIPHANY

"Behold there came wise men from the East."—
St. Matt. 2:1.

I. THE CALL OF THE CHRIST-CHILD.

1. It is of the nature of love to demand
an object upon which to lavish itself.
The human heart ever desires something
to which it can in outward expression
devote itself. The Sacred Heart of the
Christ-Child was no exception, for His
was a true human heart. Consider the
Heart of the Infant Jesus yearning toward
His people, calling them to come to Him
that He might bestow upon them the
rich gifts of His love.

2. Consider the love of the Christ-
Child, as wide as the world. He called
the Shepherds, His own race according
to the flesh; but His love is not satisfied.
He sends a mysterious message across the

world. Heart speaks to heart, and in
their distant land the Gentile Kings hear
His summons. The star confirms the
inward call of love, and leaving all they
follow the mystic leading.

3. How like to the Shepherds are
these holy Kings! We know nothing of
their antecedents. Their previous history is a blank, but the first word we
hear of them is of a mysterious message
from God, a flaming guide in the midnight sky, and their hearts all the while
waiting, ready, attuned to hear the divine
voice. Then swift obedience, a mighty
faith in perplexity, and the reward of
sharing the worship of the Incarnate
God.

II. THE PREPARATION OF THE MAGI.

1. As with the Shepherds of Bethlehem, all things point to what their spiritual history had been. We can trace it as
surely as men read the planet's history
in the rocks. In some far off land, out-

side the covenant of Israel, they had
known a divine leading. They followed
their light. They did their best. They
groped after God, if haply they might
find Him. They had but little. To this
little they were true.

2. No promises were given them.
They had no hint of any unusual revelation, no keen and sustaining anticipa-
tion of a voice, a sign. They knew of no
high reward awaiting them in this world
or in the next. They were faithful to
God for His own sake and not for a reward for which they hoped.

3. They did not suspect the divine
purpose in this preparation. But all the
while the Eternal Mind had planned that
they should be the first Gentiles to come
to the brightness of His rising. They
were able to fulfil their vocation because
they were faithful to the progressive
steps of the preparation as God led them
on little by little. Only by like faith-

fulness shall we be meet to fulfil the divine predestination for us. What step does He call me to take to-day? Am I daily seeking to find out His purpose for me?

THE JOURNEY OF THE MAGI

"Behold there came wise men from the East to Jerusalem saying, Where is He that is born King of the Jews?"—St. Matt. 2:1, 2.

I. THE PERPLEXITY OF THE WISE MEN.

1. The inner voice, confirmed by the guiding star, had led them far from home. They cared not whither it led, if it would but guide them to their King. They sacrificed friends, home, position, all to fulfil their vocation. God gives me guidance; He makes my duty clear, but I draw back.

2. Behold God honouring His Church. As they drew near to the Holy City He withdraws the light, for here the voice of the Church was to be heard. The chief priests and the scribes sat in Moses' seat; their voice was that of the living Church. God hushes the inner voice, and the

glittering star no longer guides, to teach them to hear the Church.

3. Consider how they stood the test. With what simple humility do these strangers inquire: "Where is He that is born King of the Jews?" Not for a moment do they doubt that the mysterious leading was true, even though now all signs fail. Nor for a moment do they doubt that the voice of the Church would answer them aright. Their faith is rewarded. They receive their reply; they follow the direction of the Church. They find the divine Child "with Mary His Mother." They are admitted into the presence of God; they enter into the Communion of Saints.

II. JOY THE FRUIT OF OBEDIENCE.

1. The interpreters of the divine oracles sent the Magi to humble little Bethlehem to find the King. They went with as much faith as though they had been conducted to the porphyry chamber

of the imperial palace; and "the star which they saw in the East went before them till it came and stood over where the young child was. And when they saw the star they rejoiced with exceeding great joy."

2. They sought Him in the King's palace; they found Him in a peasant's stable. But they hesitated not. "They fell down and worshipped Him." They needed not the outward trappings of royalty to convince them that He was their King. They had been true to the inner light, and the witness of their hearts did not fail them now. My Lord keeps tryst with me in the humble places, in every lowly happening of my daily life. But only through faithfulness in ordinary things can I hear His voice, can I see His face.

3. In their spiritual desolation the wise men had sought to God. Perplexity, instead of discouraging them, only made

them the more zealous in their quest.
Their reward was that of them who hold
fast by Him in spiritual dryness, even
when His face seems turned away from
them.   Fear not, the light of His counte-
nance will shine once more.   "Wait for
it, because it will surely come, it will not
tarry" (Hab. 2:3).

THE GIFTS OF THE MAGI

"And when they had opened their treasures, they presented unto Him gifts; gold and frankincense and myrrh."—St. Matt. 2:11.

I. THE SPIRIT OF THE GIFTS.

1. "All things come of Thee, O Lord, and of Thine own have we given Thee" (I Chron. 29:14). We can give nothing to God which we did not first receive from Him. In one sense they cost us nothing. All offerings made to Him are therefore to be symbolic of the inner dedication of self to His service. My Epiphany offerings are worthless unless they are the expression of the gold of a consecrated heart, the incense of humble prayer, and the myrrh of loving patience in all suffering and in mortification of my will.

2. In another sense my offerings may cost me much. They may be the ex-

pression of a real sacrifice, and they are indeed of no avail if this be not so. What does the service I give to God cost me? Recall the words of David: "Neither will I offer burnt offerings unto the Lord my God of that which doth cost me nothing" (II Sam. 24:24). Often that which is required of me day by day accords with my natural tastes. It might easily be a more real sacrifice to give up a certain service in which I now find satisfaction.

3. Nevertheless, such satisfaction does not impair, but rather enhances the value of my offerings, provided I refer it also to God, making an additional offering of my natural taste and inclination, dedicating to Him "all that I am and all that I have." Joy in sacrifice is a gift of God, and is indicative of His acceptance of my offering, and He would not accept it if my spirit were amiss. So the sense of burden, the pressure of pain in service, should fill us with a grateful joy. Our Lord said:

"My yoke is easy and my burden is light," and "ye shall find rest unto your souls"; but He not the less meant us to realize it as a yoke and a burden, sweet to bear because borne for Him.

II. The Meaning of the Gifts.

1. Gold, the most precious offering they could bring. The value of a thing is indicated by the price paid for it by intelligent buyers in the open market. My soul was bought with the price of the life of the Son of God; and this price was willingly paid by Him Who knows perfectly the value of all things. I must lay this precious thing, my own soul and life, at the feet of the infant Jesus, and make it the special business of my life to watch lest I take back from Him, even in the least degree, that which I have given Him.

2. Frankincense. In this offering the Magi declared the Deity of the Holy

Child, and so the Blessed Mother and St. Joseph must have understood; for they would have resisted the sacrilege of offering incense to any but God. (See Exod. 30:37, 38). Thus did the Gentile strangers declare Him to be God Who had come to His own, and His own received Him not. He has come very nigh unto me, even into my heart. The providential ruling of His Hand appears each hour of my life. Do I recognize Him, and with the Magi worship Him?

3. Myrrh, the symbol of suffering and mortification. Myrrh offered Him as a Baby in the manger; myrrh offered Him on the day of His burial. From Bethlehem to Calvary He was a man of sorrows and acquainted with grief. Is the disciple above his Master? "If any man will come after Me, let him take up his cross." The gold of a precious soul is but dross unless it be perfumed with the myrrh of His Passion, unless it bear the "marks of

the Lord Jesus." The incense of prayer is an abomination to God if not offered with the myrrh of a mortified spirit, a broken and contrite heart.

THE FLIGHT INTO EGYPT

"Arise, and take the young Child and His Mother and flee into Egypt."—St. Matt. 2:13.

I. THE DREAM OF JOSEPH.

1. Consider the dream of the first Joseph. His dream of power and sovereignty was the cause of his exile into Egypt that he might save his brethren by a great deliverance (Gen. 45:7). Compare it with the dream of St. Joseph, warned to flee into Egypt with the Holy Child that He might be preserved for the salvation of His brethren. In the one case the salvation of Israel according to the flesh; in the other, the salvation of the true Israel of God in every age and clime. In both cases the manifestation of the protecting Love of God for the people He longed to save.

2. Consider the circumstances of the Flight; the sudden midnight rousing of

the Mother and Child; no time for explanations; fleeing away in the darkness; the terror lest pursuit should overtake them; the trembling fear at every passing traveller. Then the silence of the desert closes about them; the great stars look down on their Creator fleeing from the cruel wrath of His creature. Yet with one breath this helpless Child could have swept His enemies into nothingness. But love works not thus. He submits; He suffers.

3. Consider my relation to the Flight. God knew of me on this night of terror. I was among those who were predestined to be saved by the Precious Blood of this Holy Child. For love of me He fled from the cruel King. He might have died for me even then, beneath the sword of Herod, but His love desired to suffer more than this for me. These infant days were but the type of the Passion for which love constrained His soul to wait. Condemned to death by Herod He went on

the way of the Cross in the wilderness.
The weary months in pagan Egypt were
a long crucifixion, cut off from His people,
a pensioner perhaps on the bounty of
strangers. And yet His love waited in
order to suffer even greater things for me.

II. Some Lessons of the Flight.

1. Meditate on the result of the
Magi's visit. The prompt answer to
God's call roused the jealous rage of
Herod, led to the massacre of the Innocents and to the Flight into Egypt of the
Holy Child. Better, men would say,
that they had remained in their Eastern
home than in bearing their witness to
bring such persecution upon innocent
victims. So the world always says.
My vocation has aroused opposition
and has occasioned sin; my conformity
to forms of Catholic worship causes
scoffers to blaspheme; my very existence
as a Christian is a standing occasion of
activity on the part of Satan, and his

servants both devils and men. But the greatest occasion of Satanic outbreak was the Incarnation itself. Should God have stayed His work of love because of these things? The follower of Christ will respond promptly, and to the utmost, to every call from God, leaving the results in His hands. He Who rules can overrule.

2. Consider the infant "martyrs in deed, though not in will," suffering for Christ. All who would live godly must suffer for Him. What have I suffered? Do I seek to find the Cross, or to eliminate the Cross? My vocation is given me just in order that I might have the opportunity to suffer for Him. If its course moves too smoothly, I must suspect my way of meeting the call. If it be a thorny path I must thank God and take courage. The happiness of Bethlehem is not for me as yet. The exile of Egypt must be endured before the heavenly Canaan and the eternal House of Bread can be mine.

3.   Consider the Wise Men returning home by another way, knowing that Herod was waiting to slay the young Child.   After this glorious season of the Nativity how many a Herod of sin is waiting to slay Christ within me.   After the spiritual effort of a great Feast we are easily off our guard, and Satan watches to take advantage of such a condition. Watch through the coming months; we have been warned of God; let us protect to our utmost the divine life within us.

THE TWO STANDARDS

"To the one we are the savour of death unto death; and to the other the savour of life unto life."
—II Cor. 2:16.

I. THE PRIESTS AND THE KING.

1. Consider the Priests at Jerusalem. Ready to point others to Christ, but not seeking Him themselves. And yet the faith of the Magi failed not. They accepted the direction of those who followed not their own doctrine, and they found the Saviour in consequence. The Church has the treasure of Divine Revelation in earthen vessels. The Minister of the Sacraments may be unworthy but none the less do these Sacraments bring us into union with God. God's love for His people will not allow that they be kept back from Him because the Minister is unworthy. The holiest priest is a

sinner, but we look not to him for help, but through him to Christ.

2. Consider the wicked king. He fears the Babe of Bethlehem lest his power be broken by a little Child. By pretending to a desire to worship, he seeks to slay Him. No surer way is there to slay the life of Christ within me than by spiritual hypocrisy. I claim Him as my Lord. I bow down and worship before Him. Is there something all the while that I am keeping back from Him? I pretend to accept His rule in my heart, and all the while my own unmortified will dominates my life.

II. THE TRUTH SEEKERS.

1. Compare the wise and humble kings of the East with the self-satisfied powers of the Church and State at Jerusalem. In their quest after Christ they sought continually to God, always ready without hesitation to follow His guiding. They followed the leading of the divinely-

sent star; they sought the synagogue when the star was withdrawn, and having found the new-born King they now sought God again regarding their return. The word "warned" implies a response given to one who had asked for help. It was their faithfulness that saved the Christ-Child, and secured time for the escape into Egypt. Prayer for guidance in every possible situation, great or small, and for readiness to follow the guidance offered,—this only will bring and keep our lives in union with God.

2. Consider the keen expectation of the distant tribes awaiting their kings' return; the eager throngs gathered about the royal pavilion to hear the news of the Infant King Who was come to redeem the world; the awe-struck tribesmen as they returned to their homes pondering these strange things in their hearts. The Magi the first preachers of Christ to the Gentiles, preparing the way for the Apostolic preaching that would be

heard a generation later throughout all the world.

3.   Consider the joy the first Apostles to these eastern tribes felt when they came to preach the Gospel and found the tradition of the Redeemer firmly fixed. We know not who were the Apostles or what were the tribes, but we know that God did not let the word sent by the Magian kings return to Him empty. Nothing I say or do for God in sincerity and love can be void of results.   He can take my weakest word and make it a thing of power, the blessed results of which only the Last Day will make known.

THE HOUSE OF BREAD

"And thou Bethlehem in the land of Juda art not the least among the princes of Juda."—St. Matt. 2:6.

I. THE EAGLES OF THE LORD.

1. "Wheresoever the body is, thither will the eagles be gathered together" (St. Luke 17:37). The word St. Luke uses means a living body. In Bethlehem lay the pure body of the Son of God, and high and valiant souls gathered for His worship. Those whose vision discerned the truth faltered not. Leaving all, suffering all, they were drawn irresistibly to His feet. Angels, Saints, shepherds from the hills, kings from far countries, these were the eagles of the Lord whose vision could pierce the veil of sense and see God Incarnate in this infant Form.

2. Jesus still lies beneath the veils of sense. On every altar, under the

forms of bread and wine, is hidden the glorified Body of the Saviour of the world. The Bread of Life, the Living Bread that came down from heaven, again dwells in the Bethlehem of His Church, the true House of Bread. Pray for the eagle-gaze of faith to know and adore Jesus with all thy heart in the Holy Sacrament. "O come, let us worship."

3. In the House of Bread He renews the strength of His people; "they shall mount up with wings as eagles, they shall run and not be weary; and they shall walk and not faint" (Isa. 40:31). It is no strength of their own that He renews, to be frittered away in the first spiritual endeavour. Under these Sacramental Veils He gives Himself, He infuses into us all the powers of His Sacred Humanity, risen, ascended, glorified. Do I fear the coming trial, the temptation? Why art thou so disquieted, O my soul? The Omnipotence of Incarnate God is thine if thou wilt but exercise it.

II. The Passports to the House of
Bread.

1. If the Altar of God is to be my
true House of Bread I must seek admit-
tance with the right dispositions. Bethlehem was crowded at this time, but men
saw not their God, they rejoiced not in
His worship; there were many weary
and heart-sore, but they found no
strength in Him. They had no faith.
"Lord, increase our faith." "Lord, I be-
lieve, help Thou mine unbelief."

2. The Hand that offers me the Bread
of Life is wounded and bleeding. My sin
wounded that Little One. Have I no
sorrow for my sin? No words of penitence as I kneel at the door? My feet
cannot touch that sacred threshold save
in penitence; until washed even in the
Precious Blood which He offers for my
strength and healing, I cannot enter in.

3. Penitence is impossible without
self-knowledge. I cannot be sorry for

what I do not know. So watchfulness over my heart, knowledge of my sins and infirmities, these alone can make me fit to kneel in the House of Bread and take into my soul the Living Bread which whoso eats shall live forever.

JANUARY 12.

LOSING AND FINDING CHRIST

"The Child Jesus tarried behind."—St. Luke
2:43.*

I. How we lose Christ out of our
Lives.

1. By mortal sin. This only can
drive Him from my heart. His love will
endure all manner of affronts, but He
cannot, without dishonouring Himself,
dwell in a heart that *deliberately* and *with
full knowledge* and *in a serious matter* (for
these are the marks of mortal sin) choses
Satan's will rather than God's will.

2. By venial sin. Small sins they
may be; dishonouring to Him, though He
tolerates them; but slight as they are,
as they increase in number, as they grow
into a fixed habit, they weaken and blind
the soul, and sooner or later mortal sin

* From the Gospel for Sunday in the Octave of the
Epiphany.

will result. Accustomed to doing Satan's will frequently in little things, some day he will demand some serious service of me, and I shall not be able to resist. The great transgression will follow, and my soul will be undone.

3. St. Charles Borromeo made a resolution never to commit deliberately even the smallest venial sin. Infirmity might overcome him, but he would not even in the smallest thing deliberately take Satan's part against God. Only in some such resolve can the soul be safe from offence against the divine love.

II. How to find Christ again.

1. St. Joseph and the Holy Mother spared themselves no pains; they returned to Jerusalem promptly. There was but one thing in all the world in their minds. This was to find Jesus again. They had not indeed lost Him through sin, for no blame was charged to them; but they sacrificed every other thought

to that of finding Him. True penitence has but one thought,—that of finding Jesus. Everything must be swept aside for the great work of penitence. Nothing else matters until Jesus be found again.

2. They sought Him sorrowing. Our sorrow must be two-fold,—(*a*) sorrow, poignant grief over our own loss, and (*b*) sorrow at the dishonour our sin has done to Him. The Prodigal Son first "came to himself," but when he realized the depth of his guilt, he said, "I will arise and go to my father."

3. The test of true sorrow for sin is amendment. A boy once defined penitence as "being sorry enough to quit." Will my penitence stand this test? But remember that amendment does not mean never committing the sin again. It means trying earnestly to do a little better every day. This is all God asks. So should we fall again, we should not be discouraged. Rise up with an Act of

Contrition. Cry for mercy, and forgiveness, and God's loving Hand will raise you up and put you once more in the path, and give you strength to persevere. He who keeps on trying cannot possibly fail in the end.

CHRIST IN THE TEMPLE

"They found Him not .. .. ..   Wist ye not that I must be about My Father's business?"— St. Luke 2: 45, 49.

I. THE LOSS OF JESUS.

1. The Gospel tells us that St. Joseph and the Blessed Mother went a day's journey not knowing that the Child had tarried behind in Jerusalem. They supposed Him to have been in the company. They took it for granted He was there. We take it for granted that He is in our hearts. I say my prayers, I make my Communions, therefore He must be within me. Am I sure? Do I examine my heart daily to make sure that I have not left Him behind?

2. "They sought Him among their kinsfolk and acquaintance," but they

found Him not. Many a man thinking
Christ to be in his heart has, when great
need came, sought Him and found Him
not even among his acquaintance. Is
He among my acquaintance? Do I
know Him? Am I known of Him? Have
I kept so fast by Him that I can turn
to Him instantly and easily in time of
spiritual need?

3.   There was nothing blameworthy in
the Blessed Mother and St. Joseph on
this occasion, for God had brought it
about to teach us the lesson that we can
take nothing for granted in our religious
life. God teaches us that He ordains
Sacraments not only as channels of grace,
but as outward signs "to assure us there-
of." The grace is not enough; He gives
me the outward and visible assurance.
The assurance of my own heart cannot
be trusted. So must the Christian soul
be ever watchful, "making his calling
and election sure."

II. The Search and the Finding.

1. Consider the anguish of the three days' search. The sense of the absence of Jesus; the bitter self-reproach; the tears and cries to God of the Blessed Mother through the long nights of desolation, praying Him to give her back her Child. Try by sympathy with the sorrows of our Holy Mother to realize what life would be without Jesus. Ask her out of her loving sympathy for poor sinners, to pray that we may ever hold fast by Him.

2. "Wist ye not that I must be about My Father's business?" Such was the response to the Blessed Mother's query. It might be considered as a rebuke were it possible to think of that Son rebuking that Mother. But God's rebukes fall on sin alone. He never rebukes human limitation or infirmity; and she was sinless. Seeing who they were, let us rather think of it as a call to a fuller grasp of the mysteries of the Incarnate Life. He had

been subject to them at Nazareth, and yet it was the Child that taught the Mother. More and more as the years of the hidden life went by, silently did He open her heart and mind to see the mystery. Now He instructs her how to draw the conclusion from the past lessons. "Wist ye not?" Does not this incident make clear so much that thou hast been taught in the past? Often we wonder at God's dealing with us. Wait in faith and patience. Some day we shall look back and see it all plainly. At this time even the Holy Mother "understood not the saying that He spake unto them." But "she kept all these sayings in her heart." Keep and ponder all that He says and does, and the light will come.

3. "Wist ye not?" Let us apply this question to ourselves, placing the emphasis on the *ye*. Long years has He lived a hidden life in our hearts. When we forgot Him, and well nigh lost Him, still

He was hidden within. He led us about and instructed us. The unceasing teaching of His Spirit has been ours. And yet we do not understand the working of His love. He says to us tenderly, yearningly, Wist *ye* not, ye of all others, ye to whom I have given so much; is it possible that ye do not understand?

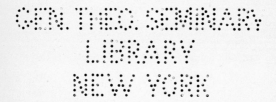

GEN. THEO. SEMINARY
LIBRARY
NEW YORK

GEN. THEO. SEMINARY
LIBRARY
NEW YORK